Original title:
The Doorway to Hope

Copyright © 2025 Creative Arts Management OÜ
All rights reserved.

Author: Simon Fairchild
ISBN HARDBACK: 978-1-80587-205-4
ISBN PAPERBACK: 978-1-80587-675-5

Pathway to Resilience

When life hands you lemons, just make pie,
Slice it up neatly, watch worries fly.
A jog on this path can make you trip,
But laughter's the sprout, that makes you skip.

The road may be bumpy, that's quite true,
But who needs a map when you've got a view?
Fallen down? Just bounce back up again,
Wearing a grin like it's your best plain.

Key to Illumination

Found a key that squeaks while it turns,
Unlocking the joy and all that it earns.
Dim rooms are fine, if you're chasing glee,
Just dance in the dark, and hum your own spree.

Lightbulbs flickering, oh what a sight,
Twinkling like stars in a pillow fight.
Grab your flashlight, let's be all aglow,
In the corners of dreams where the wild things grow.

Foyer of Fresh Starts

In the foyer of fresh starts, I take off my shoes,
Scuffing the floor, leave behind the blues.
With a flourish I twirl, and fall on my face,
But a chuckle escapes in this silliness space.

New beginnings are like socks gone awry,
One striped, one polka-dot, oh me, oh my!
Yet in this cozy nook, I trace my own path,
With puns in my pocket and laughter to bath.

Threshold of Light

This threshold of light, with a welcome so wide,
In shadows I slipped, but now here's my ride.
I jump through the beam, it sparkles and glows,
While tripping on laughter, oh where did it go?

With shades on my nose, I swagger and strut,
Dancing through rays like a swaying butt.
So here's to the brightness, so silly and bright,
Igniting our hearts, not just the night.

Harbor of Healing

In a harbor where laughter sails,
Seagulls act like curious jails.
A kayak named 'Feel Better' floats,
With ice cream cones for captain's coats.

Bubbles pop with each silly wave,
Pinching toes, that's how we behave.
Sailboats tip, but we won't drown,
Just giggles and grins in this town.

Bridge to Brilliance

Across a bridge of jelly beans,
Rainbow trolls in silly scenes.
They juggle dreams, one by one,
Underneath the giggling sun.

Each step brings a marshmallow tale,
With unicorns that never fail.
Brilliance shines from quirky stars,
With laughter echoing from afar.

Entrance of Encouragement

An entrance framed in candy canes,
With jokes that dance in silly strains.
Knock once, and a dragon appears,
Spitting out marshmallow cheers.

With each jest, the door swings wide,
Offering hugs and a joyful ride.
Where frowns turn upside down like charts,
And giggles fluff the bouncing hearts.

Arch of Infinite Chances

Beneath an arch of giggles bright,
Where pumpkins cartwheel in delight.
Turtles wearing party hats,
Crack the code and make us chat.

Every chance is like a pie,
With silly flavors that make you sigh.
So take a risk, the cake is sweet,
In layers of laughter, life's a treat.

Harbor of Aspiration

In a boat made of dreams, we sail so bright,
With oars made of laughter, we row through the night.
The fish tell us jokes, the stars wink and sway,
We anchor in giggles, at the end of the day.

The tides bring us hopes, like candy from shore,
We dance with the waves, who could ask for more?
A seagull drops puns, like treasures to find,
In this harbor of wishes, we're all intertwined.

Portal of Unseen Blessings

A door with no handle, just a smile and a grin,
It opens with kindness, bringing joy from within.
What's behind this strange portal? Do dare to explore!
A parade of bad puns shakes hands at the door.

Rainbows stretch giggles from ceiling to floor,
With cats playing chess, and clowns keeping score.
Invisible gifts, like balloons in the sky,
As we stumble through laughter, we soar, oh my!

Gateway to Unraveled Fears

A gate made of whimsy, it creaks and it whines,
With ghosts that just giggle and jump on the lines.
Fear wears silly hats and dances on air,
We trip over chuckles and float without care.

The monsters of doubt wear socks that don't match,
They're juggling rubber chickens, quite the fine catch!
With a tickle of courage, we push open wide,
And step into silliness, arms open, we glide.

Entrance of Unfurling Wings

With a flap and a flutter, the door swings ajar,
Behind it, a chorus of whimsical bazaar.
Wings made of paper, and chatter so sweet,
We dance with the breezes, our hearts skip a beat.

In this realm of delight, we take off like kites,
With giggles for fuel, we soar through the nights.
Clouds are our pillows, the sun shines our way,
In this entrance of joy, we never delay.

Axis of Light

In the hall where shadows play,
A lightbulb flickers, come what may.
It dances round in a silly spree,
Knocking over my cup of tea.

A cat joins in with a mighty leap,
To chase the light, a secret to keep.
But all it does is bump the floor,
And leave me laughing, wanting more.

Conduit of Change

There's a mailbox with a silly grin,
Collecting hopes, just throw them in!
Each letter's filled with dreams to speak,
Yet most are just my lunch next week.

The postman trips, it's quite a show,
Delivering joy with a toe-to-toe.
He waves goodbye in a clumsy dance,
Here's to mail, and my next chance!

Entrance to New Adventures

A garden gate swings with a squeak,
Beyond it, treasures that I seek.
I hear the giggle of flowers bright,
Inviting me to what feels just right.

A frog amidst petals, jumps so bold,
Telling tales of adventures untold.
With each hop, a mystery to crack,
As I follow the frog, there's no turning back!

Paved Path to Tomorrow

A sidewalk leads to who knows where,
With gum stuck tight to my shoe, beware!
Every step bounces, each crack a laugh,
As squirrels race by, in their own hot bath.

There's a sandbox that dreams of the sea,
Building castles, just you and me.
Tomorrow's here, and what a sight,
To laugh our way into the night!

Invitation to Belief

Knock, knock! Who's there? Just me,
A tiny hope, as bright as a pea.
Can you believe in a smile so wide?
Or a penguin that learns how to glide?

With every giggle, dreams take flights,
Like squirrels on scooters, in silly tights.
Laughter's the key, so let's not defame,
Finding joy in the most ridiculous game.

So polish your shoes and bring your cheer,
It's time to chase away every fear.
Bouncing on clouds, let's reach for the moon,
With ice cream cones, we'll all be in tune.

So enter this space with a wink and a grin,
Let's dance through the chaos, let the fun begin!
Happiness waits, no need to delay,
In this zany place, we'll find our way!

Passageway to Joy

Step right up, don't be shy,
Where laughter floats and giggles fly.
A parade of puppies in tiny hats,
Join the fun, no time for spats!

With marshmallow clouds and candy canes,
We'll make a ruckus as laughter reigns.
Bouncing on bunnies, what a sight,
Chasing rainbows, we'll feel the light.

Kites with sunglasses soar in the air,
Even the grumpiest can't help but care.
In this place of whimsy, all hearts will sway,
Sharing joy like popcorn on a sunny day.

So grab your cap, tightly secure,
Through this tunnel, you'll feel pure.
Let's trip on giggles and tumble with glee,
In this passageway, we're all truly free!

Portal of Growth

Let's plant some seeds of laughter today,
With dreams that wiggle and bounce all the way.
A garden of thoughts, both silly and wild,
Where giggles sprout, and grown-ups feel like a child.

Sprinkle some joy like fairy dust,
Watch it blossom into a must.
Frogs in top hats will join the fun,
Growing tall under the shining sun.

Pinch of hilarity, a dash of delight,
Watch us blossom from morning to night.
Dancing daisies and snickering trees,
Laughter so loud it can tickle a breeze.

In this portal where chuckles reside,
Together we flourish, side by side.
So grab a spade, dig in full throttle,
Let's cultivate laughter, fill up the bottle!

Lantern of Aspiration

Shiny lanterns, flicker and glow,
Guiding the way where silly thoughts flow.
Bubbles of giggles in a whimsical whirl,
Each dream takes flight; let's give it a twirl!

With mounting mirth, like a comedy show,
We'll laugh 'til we can't, then let our smiles grow.
Hop on the merry-go, ride 'til we're sore,
Discovering aspirations we've never explored.

Silly hats and shoes two sizes too big,
Dance to the rhythm of a twerpy jig.
Aim for the stars that shoot like confetti,
Where aspirations linger, all sparkly and pretty.

So lift your lantern, bright as can be,
Let's light up the world; come and see!
In this gleeful place, our dreams feel alive,
With laughter and hope, we'll surely thrive!

Gateway of Heartfelt Dreams

In a land where wishes slide,
A giant door swings open wide.
With socks on hand and moons in tow,
We trip and stumble, but still we glow.

Each foot we place, a joke unfolds,
Chasing fortune, never too bold.
Rabbits dance in top hats, too,
They wink at me, 'We're here for you!'

Laughter echoes through the halls,
Tickling toes in marble stalls.
Carpets fly, we ride and cheer,
On broomsticks made of gummy beer.

So step right up, don't mind the mess,
In this realm of dreams, there's no stress.
The floor may quake, the walls may sway,
But smiles abound in this silly fray.

Stoop of Surrender

On the stoop where giggles grow,
A weathered broom begins to flow.
It sweeps away my doubt and strife,
 Bringing forth the joy of life.

With lemonade and sunny days,
We dance in clogs, in funny ways.
A cat in shades strums on the fence,
Each note a joke, it all makes sense.

The mailman trips, he grabs his hat,
A dancing dog sings, 'What of that?'
Laughter fills the cool, sweet air,
As we find bliss in simple care.

So come and join this playful spree,
Where even ducks can dance with glee.
The stoop may creak, but hearts take flight,
In this laughter, everything's right.

Embrace of New Horizons

At dawn's embrace, the sun appears,
With coffee brewed and lots of cheers.
A parrot yells, 'Up with the day!'
As I trip on my slippers, 'Hooray!'

The horizon's bright, a vast delight,
With toucans sporting shades so bright.
They squawk about the fun ahead,
While I munch on toast and jam spread.

Each step I take, a dance I find,
With squirrels grooving, I'm so inclined.
The flowers grin, with colors bold,
Whispering secrets, tales retold.

So wave goodbye to clouds of gray,
For every mishap is just play.
With laughter loud and hearts so free,
New horizons call, come sing with me!

Ledger of Life's Potential

In a ledger filled with dreams galore,
Sticky notes mark all that I adore.
Counting giggles, crafting schemes,
In this wild life, we chase our dreams.

With rubber chickens and pie-filled carts,
We tally joy; it's how it starts.
Balloons float high, a kite in tow,
Swinging and laughing, we pretty flow.

The numbers dance, they twist and shout,
With every flub, we find new routes.
Lattes spilled and cookies munch,
Life's potential in every crunch.

So write it down, each silly act,
In our ledger, we find the tact.
For even mischief can inspire,
The funniest tales never tire.

Arch of New Horizons

Under the arch, where dreams get a shove,
You might find a pig that learned to fly above.
Clouds tickle your nose, it's a silly affair,
Giggling daisies dance, a quirky debonair.

Laughter spills out like a bubbling brook,
Even the trees turned and gave us a look.
Stars wear sunglasses, the moon's in a hat,
Let's hop on a whim, and how about that!

Bridge to Light's Embrace

There's a bridge made of jellybeans, colorful and bright,
Swaying with laughter, a most curious sight.
Rabbits in bowties dance with such flair,
Tickling each other without a care.

Beneath it, the river hums nonsense and cheer,
While fish throw a party, inviting you near.
Giggling trees throw confetti of leaves,
Who knew such silliness life truly believes!

Pathway Rooted in Faith

On a pathway paved with candy and dreams,
Socks turn to sandals—oh, how it seems!
With each silly step, shiny gumdrops unfold,
A penguin in glasses tells secrets retold.

Hopes sprout like daisies, all crooked and neat,
While marshmallow clouds provide cushions for feet.
Sometimes you stumble, and that's quite okay,
Just bounce back up, and laugh all the way!

Passage to Healing Waters

Through a passage of bubbles, we splash and we giggle,
Rubber duck armies in a serious wiggle.
The water sings songs of belly laughs bright,
It's a wacky adventure beneath twinkling lights.

Here, worries dissolve like ice cream on sun,
Dancing with dolphins, oh, isn't this fun?
Riding the waves with a grin ear to ear,
In this joyful journey, there's nothing to fear!

Promenade of Possible Futures

In a world of might-have-beens,
I tripped over my own feet,
Laughing at the paths unworn,
Chasing cats that can't be beat.

Juggling dreams like clumsy clowns,
I bumped into a friendly chair,
It whispered tales of upside-downs,
While I wondered where's my hair?

They say the road to glory's paved,
With puddles filled with hopes and jest,
Each splatter drips with dreams enslaved,
Yet here I am, still on my quest.

So come, let's dance in silly shoes,
With every twirl, we'll spin a chance,
For futures bright with vibrant hues,
Where laughter leads the way to dance.

Oasis of Optimistic Reflections

In a desert rich with lemonade,
We sip sunshine from a glass,
While cacti wear their sun-block shade,
And tumbleweeds just love to pass.

Mirages giggle in the heat,
As visions shimmer, stretch, and tease,
I chase the sand without my feet,
But find my toes in windy breeze.

Here in this patch of silly shade,
Where every laugh's a kite in flight,
We plant the seeds of wacky trade,
And harvest joy, both day and night.

So take a sip and join the fun,
As donkeys dance with hats askew,
In this oasis, we have won,
A paradise for me and you.

Portico of Serendipity

At the entryway to blissful chance,
I tripped on laughter's slippery tile,
Where pigeons plot a silly dance,
And trees wear smiles that go a mile.

The winds are filled with chatter heed,
As robins share their morning news,
I plant a wish, it sprouts a seed,
And grows into a pair of shoes.

With every step, a giggle blooms,
Unlikely pals, all in a row,
We skip through corridors and rooms,
Where every whim ignites the glow.

So let's embrace the chaos bright,
With hats adorned in mismatched flair,
For in this portico of light,
We find our joy beyond compare.

Avenue of Hope

Amidst the cracks, a cat sits proud,
Dreams of tuna, meows so loud.
Bicycles whizzing, kids in tow,
Chasing rainbows where wildflowers grow.

A squirrel skates, oh what a sight,
Stealing snacks, then dashing out of fright.
Laughter blooms, with every cheer,
In this place, my worries disappear.

Sidewalks twist, like curly fries,
Hope's mailbox filled with funny lies.
A letter here, a joke to share,
Like piñatas bursting with fresh air.

At every turn, a twist in plot,
A rubber chicken, why not, why not?
Under the sun, our laughter floats,
In this avenue, joy is what promotes.

Doorframe of Freedom

A door swings wide, a circus awaits,
Acrobats tumble, defying fates.
The sign reads 'Welcome,' but don't you stare,
Inside, there's a duck wearing a pear!

Juggling dreams, with socks on their hands,
The clowns take charge, making wild plans.
Laughter bubbles, like soda on ice,
Freedom sparkles, oh, isn't it nice?

Wobbly tightropes, no safety net,
A chicken comes in, without a regret.
She struts her stuff, a grand parade,
When life gives you lemons, make lemon aid!

With pies in the air, we dance and sing,
In this frame, happiness is the King.
Here, troubles shrink, like socks in a wash,
Embrace the chaos, give life a toss!

Opening for the Awakened Heart

An open door with a cosmic twist,
Is that a cupcake? I can't resist!
The universe winks, with frosting fair,
Inviting me in, without a care.

Inside are dreams, in colors bright,
A disco ball spins, oh what a sight!
With every beat, my heart does sway,
Dancing like jelly, in a golden ray.

Whispers of wisdom, with a giggle or two,
The tea is sweet, with a dash of blue.
Cards promising fortune, like glittered stars,
While martinis are shaken—here are no bars!

As wishes take flight, like balloons on a string,
Happiness smiles, oh, what joy it brings!
In this opening, paths intertwine,
With giggles galore, life's simply divine.

Path of Faith

A path so quirky, it zigzags 'round,
With rubber ducks, all wearing crowns.
Socks on the line, flappin' with glee,
A parade of giggles is all I see!

Banana peels, oh what a slip!
Dodging the chaos, it's quite a trip.
Grapes pontificate on their wise way,
Singing old songs of a joyful play.

Each goofy step, a dance of fate,
A marching band made of gummy bears' weight.
With sprinkles and laughter, the road is wide,
In this silly land, we take it in stride.

Faith shines bright, like a neon sign,
With every chuckle, our hearts align.
So skip and twirl, embrace the fun,
On this path, it's all just begun!

Entrance to Renewal

When life gives you lemons, make a drink,
But don't forget to add a little wink.
A door swings open, laughter starts,
With goofy hats, we play our parts.

The floor may creak, but so do we,
Dance like nobody's watching, set it free.
A silly wig on a serious man,
Renewal begins with a light-hearted plan.

With each new step, we trip and fall,
But giggles echo, we'll stand tall.
Together we stumble, together we play,
As the door creaks wide, brighter the day.

So bring your quirks, your silly ways,
In this grand entrance where laughter stays.
Life's a jest, a whimsical spree,
Join the fun, come dance with me!

Passage into Radiant Futures

We marched through clouds, oversized shoes,
In our minds, we chase the whimsical blues.
Contraptions here, gadgets galore,
A future that's bright, but strange at the core.

With roller-skates tied to our feet,
We glide and we stumble, oh, what a treat!
Pizza delivery on a pogo stick,
This future's crazy, come take a pick!

Flying fish and dancing bears,
With every corner, a new surprise ensnares.
We're poking through the fabric of dreams,
Life's a giggle, or so it seems.

Laugh at the chaos, embrace the ride,
In the passageway where wonders collide.
Let's twirl into tomorrows, come what may,
With humor as our guide, we're here to stay!

Portal of Resilient Hearts

Through the portal, we march with care,
Silly faces and not a single stare.
Resiliency wrapped in rainbow bands,
We tackle troubles with juggling hands.

When the world feels heavy, don a crown,
In our own kingdom, we'll never frown.
Defying gravity, we float like balloons,
With laughter as our favorite tunes.

The heart can bounce, it can spring,
Even in gloom, we make it sing.
Dancing through rain, with puddles to spot,
Life's a circus, and we're tied in a knot.

So join hands tight, with giggles in the air,
In the portal of life, joy's everywhere.
With resilient spirits, let laughter impart,
Together we shine with our funny hearts!

Veiled Entrance to Joy

Beneath a curtain of giggles and cheer,
Lies a space where laughter's crystal clear.
The veils may flutter, the lights may spin,
But stepping through builds the joy within.

Socks mismatched, bright colors collide,
In this whimsical space, there's nowhere to hide.
The serious faces fade with the mist,
A dance floor where troubles simply can't exist.

With a kazoo chorus, we raise our voice,
In the entrance of glee, we rejoice!
Silly hats worn like crowns on our heads,
In this kingdom of laughter, no tears are shed.

So tiptoe through joy, with a hop and a skip,
In the veiled entrance, don't forget your quip.
Together we'll twirl, we'll shimmy and sway,
In this realm of delight, come play all day!

Passage of Patience

In a place where time does zip,
Socks are lost on every trip.
The clock's hands dance a jolly jig,
While I just search for lost old swig.

I wait for trains that never come,
Palms sweating like the overcooked gum.
A pigeon coos, as if in jest,
While I just wish for time to rest.

Hours crawl, like snails on stage,
Each tick and tock, a brand new page.
But in this maze of slow delight,
Patience will surely wear a light.

So here I stand with grin quite wide,
To find the joy in this slow ride.
With giggles, maps, and a frown or two,
Oh patience, thank you for the view!

Stairway to the Future

Up the steps, I take a peek,
What awaits, a chance to speak?
But wait, a cat blocks my way,
Strutting like it owns the day.

Each stair creaks like an old joke,
With every step, I hear it poke.
A robot hand with snacks in tow,
Offers chips, a tasty show.

Future bright with pixel lights,
But first, I dodge those silly bites.
A floor made out of rainbow beams,
Who knew the future was this gleam?

So I skip to where laughter flows,
Through time with friends, where humor glows.
The future's bright, with chuckles sweet,
A stairway lined with tasty treats!

Lattice of Liveliness

In a garden of giggles and glee,
Vines dance and sway, oh look at me!
A lattice woven with joy and cheer,
Where even the weeds have jokes to share.

Bumblebees buzz with a silly tune,
Dancing under the goofy moon.
Flowers sneeze in colors so bright,
A riot of laughter in the night.

The sunbeams tickle the trees so stout,
Branches wave like buddies, no doubt.
A patch of grass with shoes that sway,
Say "Hi!" to the clouds, on this fine day!

Here in this maze of merry sprout,
Liveliness rules, there's never a doubt.
So kick off your shoes, come join the fun,
In this lively garden, everyone's won!

Gate of Gratitude

A gate swings wide, just with a grin,
Behind it lies all the fun within.
Thanks to pizza, and friends galore,
Laughter echoing from every door.

Sticky notes say "You rock!" a lot,
Reminders of joy that can't be bought.
I trip on gratitude like a shoe,
And laugh 'cause my socks are mismatched too!

With every hug and smile I thread,
Gratitude blooms and lightly spreads.
It's a giggle fest at this fine gate,
Where thankful hearts congregate.

So step right up, no time for rue,
Gratitude's waiting, just for you.
With pie, and puns, life's a playful spree,
Let's celebrate us, and just be free!

Walkway of Cherished Visions

Life's a path of quirky flair,
With rubber chickens everywhere.
Step right up, don't be shy,
Silly hats will make you fly!

Rainbows dance on shoes so bright,
As we twirl into the night.
Take a leap, give it a spin,
A giggle hides where dreams begin!

Each step's a hop, a joyful shout,
Weirdos in and out, no doubt!
Bouncing through bizarre delight,
Stay up late and sleep till light.

Grab a friend, don't be a bore,
Sing and laugh, then sing some more.
With every wiggle, every cheer,
We chase away the doubt and fear!

Underpinning of Hopeful Horizons

In the land where socks don't match,
We find the dreams we love to hatch.
Waffles fly and giggles zoom,
Every corner holds a room!

Sideways smiles and silly faces,
Dance and laugh through all the spaces.
Jellybeans rain from the skies,
For every frown, a bounce will rise!

Chasing butterflies in hats,
Dancing with the cuddly cats.
Laughing hard till bellies ache,
All it takes is one small break!

Through the silliness, we glide,
Wandering with arms spread wide.
In this chaos, joy aligns,
Hope's bright spark forever shines!

Threshold to the Unseen

Open wide, a door appears,
Filled with laughter, jokes, and cheers.
Expect the odd, the twisty turns,
Where every heart and belly churns!

Flip-flops squeak on floors of gold,
Tales of mischief will unfold.
Curly fries and soda fountains,
Joy awaits from hidden mountains!

Jokingly we dance with fate,
Silly baboons consider fate.
Peanut butter on the wall,
Is that the best way to enthral?

Step beyond, where dreams collide,
In this madness, we can hide.
With chuckles sweet and pranks galore,
The unseen world provides much more!

Sanctuary of New Light

Where the sunbeam's dance and play,
Squirrels wear a bow tie today!
Bouncing with a smile so wide,
Adventure waits on every side!

Snuggled deep in fluffy cloud,
We laugh and sing, we're feeling loud.
Banana peels on every floor,
Careful now, you might hit the door!

Whimsical whispers greet us near,
As we spin and sip our cheer.
Lollipop trees grow tall and strong,
In this place, we all belong!

Hope shines bright like neon lights,
In this sanctuary of delights.
With every giggle, every tease,
We find our spirits soaring free!

Staircase to Serenity

Climbing stairs with squeaky shoes,
Each step a giggle, who knew?!
A handrail's dance, a twist and spin,
On this staircase, laughter's a win!

A cat nearby rolls down with grace,
Chasing shadows, a silly race.
I trip and tumble, land on my back,
Even the air here gives me a whack!

A ceiling fan spins in delight,
Whispering jokes in the soft moonlight.
With every thud, I chuckle loud,
Searching for peace in a giggle crowd.

At the top, I find a sign,
"Welcome to fun, where worries decline."
With humor as my guide today,
I leave my troubles, come what may!

Frame of New Beginnings

A canvas brush with colors bright,
Stating boldly, "I'm alright!"
Swirls of past laugh at my flaws,
My masterpiece extends applause!

Glancing at frames with goofy poses,
Billy-goat grins and wiggly noses.
Taking selfies with silly glee,
Every click, a new decree.

Pencil in hand, I sketch my fate,
Dancing elephants, oh what a date!
With every line, there's laughter shared,
Creating joy, I'm unprepared!

In the gallery, smiles abound,
New beginnings spin round and round.
With every chuckle, I do declare,
Life's a canvas, fun and rare!

Entrance to Inspiration

Knocking at doors of wild ideas,
With funny hats and oversized gears.
"Who's there?" shouts the brain in mine,
"Just a pickle in a polka-dot line!"

Inside awaits a zany crew,
A dog who raps and a cat in a shoe.
They welcome me with jokes galore,
"Step right in! We've got more!"

Ideas bounce like rubber balls,
Making silly sounds within these walls.
I trip on thoughts, they roll away,
Bringing laughter to this bright display.

An "aha!" moment with a little jig,
I dance like no one's watching, so big!
This entrance leads to wild new schemes,
Filled with laughter and whimsical dreams!

Vista of Optimism

From the hilltop, what a view,
Bouncing bunnies, and a dancing shoe.
Clouds shaped like ice cream cones,
Chirping birds with silly tones!

Each laugh echoes, a sound divine,
Sipping lemonade, feeling fine.
With every chuckle, troubles fade,
In this vista, peace cascades!

A slide of joy, a swing of cheer,
Friends gathered, spreading good here.
We play hide and seek with the sun,
In this land, we all are one.

Mountains of joy, valleys of glee,
Waving to silliness: "Oh, come see!"
With each glance, I raise a toast,
To the funny moments, we love the most!

Threshold of Tomorrow

I found a door that led me here,
It creaked and squeaked, what's this I hear?
A land of socks that never match,
And talking cats that love to scratch.

I asked a frog what time is it,
He said, "Just hop, don't lose your wit!"
With every leap, my worries blend,
Who knew the future could be a friend?

The key was lost, it slipped away,
But laughter leads, so here I play.
A dance with fate, a silly jig,
In this strange land, I'm now a gig!

So here's my toast to what's ahead,
With rubber chickens, mischief spread.
For in this world, the best of schemes,
Are made from wacky, wild dreams!

Gateway to Infinite Light

I stumbled on a portal bright,
It flashed and blinked, oh what a sight!
With puppies bounding, tails all wag,
They carried snacks in every bag.

A sign said, "Welcome, bring your cheer!"
So I confessed my pizza fear.
The cheese replied with a cheesy grin,
"Have a slice, just dive right in!"

Balloons that giggle floated by,
While sunbeams danced from sky to pie.
A tug of war with a wild kite,
In this realm, wrong feels so right!

So if you find this quirky space,
Don't fret your frown, don't hide your face.
For every chuckle leads the way,
To brighter tomorrows, come what may.

Passageway of Possibilities

I walked along a funky hall,
Where every door could lead to thrall.
A penguin served me tea and cake,
He said, "Step in, for goodness sake!"

There were no rules in sight, it seems,
Just quirky folks and wild daydreams.
A llama wearing fancy pants,
Invited me to take a chance!

With each new door a fresh surprise,
A monkey wearing hats so wise.
He pitched a game of monkey ball,
Within this space, we'd never fall!

So grab your hat and hold on tight,
Adventure calls, the world's so bright!
Through every turn, a grin will glow,
In this grand maze of "yes, let's go!"

Beyond the Veil of Despair

Beyond the gloom, a sparkle flashed,
With giggles sweet, all worry dashed.
A dragon baked me cookies warm,
In this place, there's little harm.

I tripped over a jester's shoe,
He laughed aloud, "What's wrong with you?"
With every tumble, joy would rise,
And silly faces filled the skies.

A turtle told me tales of glee,
Of turtles racing—who'd believe?
He winked and said, "Just take your time,
The best things grow amidst the rhyme!"

So leave the frown, embrace the cheer,
For here, my friend, there's naught to fear.
With every chuckle through the fray,
You'll find the light's not far away!

Threshold of Vibrant Whispers

In the hall of giggles, I stand tall,
A doorknob glimmers, inviting us all.
Whispers of joy, carried on a breeze,
Hope wears bright colors, aiming to please.

Balloons float by with a silly grin,
They say, 'Open wide, let the fun begin!'
With each twist of fate, laughter examines,
Even the cat joins, sporting large shamans.

Through vibrant chatter, the world feels light,
Turning dread into laughter, like fire to bright.
Step through, my friend, leave worries behind,
In this cheerful realm, happiness you'll find!

So strike up a joke, invite in the zest,
Here, joy is the rule, and you are the guest.
With a wink and a smile, let your heart soar,
At this threshold of whispers, you'll always want more!

Gateway of Unwritten Stories

A portal of giggles, nothing but cheer,
Stories untold dance, all drawing near.
We'll pen our adventures, grab life with glee,
In this wild scrapbook, just you and me.

With markers and crayons, let's outline our dreams,
A castle of candy, or so it seems.
Each stroke brings magic, a tale you can wear,
With ice cream and laughter, nothing can compare.

Let's leap into shadows, hang upside down,
In the theater of delights, we wear every crown.
Imaginations buzzing like bees on a quest,
In this gateway of stories, we'll never rest!

So grab hold of whimsy; let's take a chance,
Turn those pages, come join the dance.
Adventure awaits, with rhymes that glow,
In this vibrant space, let your story flow!

Door of Rejuvenation

Here lies a door, painted bright and bold,
With squeaks and giggles, welcome, behold!
Turn the handle, give it a shake,
What lies beyond? A joyfully baked cake!

In colorful gardens of chocolate delight,
Frogs wear top hats, all set for a flight.
Bounce on the clouds—made of marshmallow fluff,
With a wink and a chuckle, we can't get enough!

Each time you open, freshness pours in,
Like a splash of bright colors, life starts to spin.
Forget the drudgery, toss it away,
In this sunshine of laughter, let's frolic and play!

So take a deep breath, feel the freedom thrive,
This door of rejuvenation keeps dreams alive.
Leap through the portal, embrace the surprise,
With giggles and sparkles, it's time to rise!

Arc of Hopeful Wishes

Under a bright rainbow, I stand with a grin,
An arc of wishes, let the fun begin!
With jellybean prayers that scatter and roll,
Let's toast to tomorrow—cheers with a bowl!

Silly dolphins dance, with bubbles galore,
Tickling the clouds, can you ask for more?
In this arc of fortune, laughter's the guide,
Every wish becomes tenfold—with giggles inside!

Hopscotch through dreams, where magic resides,
Fly high on balloons, with fate as our rides.
With each leap of hope, our spirits will soar,
In this whimsical world, we'll always explore!

So join in the fiesta, where dreams take flight,
In this arc of wishes, everything's light.
With a wink and a wiggle, let's dance in delight,
At the end of the rainbow, it's all out of sight!

Portal of Promising Paths

A portal appeared, quite out of the blue,
Right next to my house, it looked like a zoo!
My cat took a leap, what trouble he'd find,
He returned with a fish and a top hat, so refined.

In socks with no holes, I pranced through the gate,
To a land made of cheese – oh, what a fate!
Rats held a council, all wearing bow ties,
They voted on snacks – a gourmet surprise!

A rabbit on stilts offered me tea,
With biscuits that danced, oh where could I be?
A dragon on wheels zoomed by with a laugh,
He quipped, "Don't you wish you had this giraffe?"

So I skipped through the portal, with giggles to spare,
Each step full of joy, each moment a dare.
If hope comes in portals, I'll keep one near me,
For life's all a circus, just wait, you'll see!

Opening to New Beginnings

An opening cracked, like a joke gone awry,
I tripped on a snail and then waved him goodbye.
Through the bright little breach in the wall of my room,
I stumbled on sunshine, a dove, and a broom.

A circus of colors swirled round in my head,
With pancakes that flew and a hat made of bread.
A gnome with a ukulele sang songs of delight,
"Your worries are silly! Now dance in the light!"

A cloud burst with giggles, like confetti in air,
As squirrels in sunglasses tossed nuts everywhere.
They said, "Come on over! Let's paint the sky blue!"
So I grabbed a few friends for a playful hullabaloo!

The opening widened, with laughter and cheer,
"Who knew that new beginnings could be so sincere?"
When life hands you jokes, just embrace the absurd,
Through comical chaos, I found my own word!

Archway of Dreams Unfolding

An archway appeared, with a wink and a grin,
I skipped through the colors as a chorus began.
Dreams danced like otters, they juggled my cares,
While marshmallows rapped from the heights of the stairs.

In slippers so fuzzy, I leapt with delight,
Chasing giggles around till the end of the night.
A turtle in shades shouted, "Race you to Mars!"
And I, with my friends, flew on chocolate bars.

The clouds played the banjo, the stars held the beat,
While unicorns stomped to the rhythm of feet.
With laughter like bubbles, we floated on high,
Together we soared, touching dreams in the sky.

In the archway of laughter, the world felt so new,
Each moment a treasure, each friend shining through.
With dreams ever folded, not quite as they seem,
We've created a journey, a wild, wacky dream!

Gateway to Brighter Skies

A gate swung wide open, a furry parade,
With penguins in tophats, oh how they paraded!
A jester flipped pancakes while twirling a kite,
He laughed, "Join the fun! What a glorious sight!"

The grass was a trampoline, bouncy and bright,
With flowers that giggled, what pure delight!
A bear with a monocle recited fine prose,
"Life's best served with laughter, this world's full of prose."

I danced with the daisies, the sun held my hand,
While breezes with laughter swept over the land.
Each shadow turned silly and twirled in the air,
It whispered, "Embrace all with joy and with flair!"

Through the gate of these skies, I felt warm and free,
With chuckles and cuddles – what could better be?
For if days are to brighten, let's fall with a sigh,
And open our hearts to the whimsy on high!

Archway of Dreams

Under a rainbow, things seem right,
Even the cats dance, what a sight!
Socks on my hands, I'm chasing my cat,
She stole my lunch, imagine that!

The clouds giggle, a ticklish breeze,
Tick-tock laughs bouncing from trees.
With squirrels in suits, strutting their stuff,
Even the squirrels think I'm too tough.

Jumping on puddles and splashing around,
A frog in a top hat leaps off the ground.
Pantomime whispers in this goofy game,
Who knew delight could be so insane?

A donut balloon floats by my side,
I wave at the fish in their little ride.
Life's a circus, and I'm the clown,
On this wild journey, I'll never frown!

Passage to Brighter Days

A banana peel slips, here I go,
Rolling to happiness, stealing the show!
The sun wears shades, all cool and bright,
While cows jump over, oh what a sight!

Lollipops growing on candy cane trees,
Butterflies laugh in a soft, warm breeze.
With marshmallow clouds and jellybean grass,
Why hurry when fun's a pig in a class?

Chocolate rivers running with glee,
I'll swim in my dreams, just wait and see!
The cows are my crew, a laugh so pure,
At the boat race with jelly, we'll surely endure!

The days are silly, the nights feel bright,
Wrapped in giggles, not a worry in sight.
In this comical land, the fun's never done,
Embrace all the chaos, let's just be one!

Portal of Renewal

In a land where socks never match,
Hedgehogs in hats, what a perfect catch!
They run a spa for the hairiest of bears,
Grooming their fur with extravagant flares.

A clock ticks backward, I'm late for my date,
With a sandwich who thinks it's quite first rate.
He tells me jokes, his bologna is grand,
For laughter and lettuce, we make quite a band!

The trees wear tutus, twirling around,
With roots that can't stop dancing on the ground.
Magic potatoes provide the best fries,
It's a feast of joy, disguised as surprise!

Jumping through portals, let's go for a ride,
With belly laughs ringing, I'm filled up with pride.
In this wacky world where giggles will glow,
We'll keep laughing forever, in laughter we flow!

Gate of Possibilities

With a hiccup and snort, I'm ready to play,
What wonders await in this goofy ballet?
A goat in a tie waves me on through,
Saying, "Join the party, we've got hot stew!"

The ducks wear bowties, quacking in tune,
Showering breadcrumbs under a cheeseball moon.
With swing sets of licorice lining the park,
We'll laugh so hard, it'll brighten the dark.

The sun sprinkles glitter from high in the sky,
While jellybeans giggle and float by.
A party of laughter, of whimsy and fun,
In this crazy place, we're never outdone!

The gate keeps swinging wide open and free,
Inviting us all to share joy endlessly.
With mischief around us, let's dance and sing,
In this land of delight, we are all the king!

Spiral of Rebirth

Round and round we go again,
With fresh socks and a hopeful grin.
Frogs can't leap, they hop instead,
Every bump on life's path, we dread.

Socks are mismatched, but who could tell?
Dancing wildly, we buzz like a bell.
We tumble through life, trip over our fate,
Laughing so loud, we just can't wait.

The cat winks at us, with a knowing stare,
As we twirl and twist without a care.
Life's a circus, pull up a chair,
Grab some popcorn; we're almost there!

Today, the sun is wearing shades,
Waving us on with its sunburned glades.
In this silly spiral, we find our way,
Tomorrow's dance is just a sway.

Beacon of Brighter Horizons

There's a lighthouse made of candy canes,
With marshmallow clouds and chocolate rains.
Out at sea, we search for a snack,
With spoons in hand, we've got no lack.

The gulls laugh at us while we munch,
Serenading our every lunch.
With jellybeans stuck in our hair,
We'll ride this wave without a care.

A rubber duck floats on by so bold,
Telling tales of adventures untold.
Each bite brings giggles, each sip a cheer,
In this silly world, there's nothing to fear.

Up over hills of whipped cream and sprinkles,
We'll slide down rainbows and giggle in twinkles.
With a heart full of joy, we soar up high,
In this sweet wonderland, we'll never say goodbye.

Entryway to Endless Possibilities

Open the fridge, what will we find?
Leftover pizza, how perfectly timed!
With a hint of hope and a sprinkle of fate,
We'll feast on delights that simply await.

In a box of mismatched socks we dive,
Wearing odd shoes makes us feel alive.
Each step is a giggle, a dance, a sway,
Life's a costume party; come on, let's play!

We bounce off walls like a rubber ball,
Chasing dreams like they're down the hall.
In this whimsical race, we're never last,
Connecting the dots with a laugh and a blast.

Oh, look! A unicorn in my kitchen's glow,
With pancakes stacked high, the syrup flows!
In this world of quirk, we're never alone,
With a heart full of laughter, we've fully grown.

Threshold of Cherished Moments

Knock, knock! Who's there? It's a silly cat,
Teasing the squirrel as it takes a spat.
On the welcome mat, there's glitter and fun,
With each little moment, joy just begun.

Playing hopscotch on rainbows and dreams,
The world is wobbly, or so it seems.
With a wink and a nod, we gather our crew,
Making memories that are all brand new.

The clock spins wildly, can't catch its breath,
Time's best friends with laughter, life, and death.
With giggles so grand and dances so bouncy,
Every tick-tock feels just like a flouncy.

So come take a peek through this door that's ajar,
It leads to a land where we all are bizarre.
With hearts full of cheer, unshackled, we roam,
In this fun frontier, we can always call home.

Curved Path of Promise

On a path that's bent and wild,
Lies a treasure, goofy and mild.
With wobbly stones and a dancing tree,
It giggles and whispers, "Come play with me!"

To the left goes a squirrel in a hat,
To the right, a cat who plays with a bat.
With every step, laughter rings clear,
Join the parade, there's nothing to fear!

A donut cloud floats overhead,
Winking at those who are filled with dread.
Grab a slice, take a leap, go ahead,
On this path, even worries are shred!

So dance with the wind; it's a great time,
With silly rhymes chased by the chime.
Every moment is sweet, do take the chance,
On this crazy, curved path of a joyful dance!

Entry of Kindling Spirits

In a hall where giggles ignite,
Happy shadows dance in the light.
With a wink and a chuckle, they come alive,
In this quirky space, feel your heart thrive.

A toaster sings while the teapot sways,
Crumpets jump in a cozy ballet.
Here, a carpet tickles your toes,
As the spirit of fun endlessly flows.

Open your heart to the whimsy near,
Find a jellybean's laugh; it's sincere!
Let silly joys fill your soul with delight,
In this entry of kindling, everything's bright.

So grab your friends, and let laughter take flight,
With confetti flying, all hearts feel light.
In this magical gathering, let spirits twirl,
In the entry of joy, give wonder a whirl!

Threshold of Abundant Light

Step through the frame; see what's in sight,
A battalion of giggles, all shining so bright.
With marshmallow clouds and candy cane rain,
Every corner's a joy, come bask in the gain!

There's a sunbeam by the cookie tree,
Offering hugs with sweet melody.
Join the dance of jolly old things,
In this vibrant place, smile as it sings!

A trampoline made of jellybeans,
Bouncing laughter bursts at the seams.
Together we'll jump, let worries take flight,
In this threshold of laughter, everything's right.

So skip on in, embrace the delight,
Where every giggle feels cozy and tight.
With a sprinkle of humor, let happiness write,
In this glorious glow, we'll ignite the night!

Passage of Infinite Beginnings

Down the passage where good vibes roam,
Ideas sparkle, calling us home.
With footnotes of fun stuck to the wall,
Chuckle your way, you'll have a ball!

A bouncing ball is our trusty guide,
Leading us forth with a whimsical stride.
Here, keys to laughter are scattered around,
Unlock all your dreams, let joy abound!

Each step feels like a festive spree,
Full of giggles like a vibrant jubilee.
With a sprinkle of magic, sparkles ignite,
In this passage of starters, we shine ever bright!

So grab a balloon, take a leap of joy,
Dance like a child, let nothing annoy.
In this space of beginnings, so gleeful and grand,
Together forever, let's make a stand!

Portal of Memories Yet to Be

In a world of socks mismatched,
I found a portal quite attached.
It led to giggles, snacks galore,
With ice cream rivers, what a score!

Past the fridge of dreams so bright,
Where leftovers dance in pure delight.
A window where the sun's a friend,
And silliness never seems to end.

In this realm, time plays a game,
Where cats wear hats and puff up fame.
With unicorns that sing and tweet,
Life tastes like cake—oh, what a treat!

I'll jump through socks to find the light,
Where laughter echoes day and night.
So wear your quirks; let them run free,
In this portal of pure glee!

Bridge Over Shadows

On a bridge of marshmallow fluff,
I skip and hop, it's just enough.
With gummy bears to hold my hand,
Together we will take a stand.

Underneath, where shadows play,
They trip and fall, then run away.
I giggle as they slip and slide,
In this wacky, vibrant ride.

Raining sprinkles from the skies,
Each drop a giggle, oh how it flies!
With every step, the world transforms,
Into a land where laughter swarms.

So wave goodbye to shadows grey,
Join the fun; don't be dismayed.
On this bridge, we find the cheer,
With silly antics drawing near!

Welcoming Embrace of Light

In the realm where tickles grow,
The light gives hugs, and so you know.
With a wink, it gives a nudge,
A giggle fits; it won't judge!

Bouncing beams like jellybeans,
They dance around in silly scenes.
Even shadows start to grin,
As laughter lifts them from within.

With every tickle of warm rays,
Old worries just begin to graze.
And every moment filled with fun,
Turns ordinary into the sun!

So take a leap and spread your joy,
Embrace the light, it's not a ploy.
In this bright world where spirits soar,
Laughter awaits; it's never a bore!

Wayfarer's Haven

In a haven made of bubble gum,
I roam with friends who laugh and run.
Adventures on a candy cloud,
Where silly thoughts are most allowed.

Here, the maps are drawn in crayon,
With trails of laughter that we stand on.
There's treasure buried in the fun,
With jokes and puns for everyone.

The compass spins in wobbly ways,
Leading us through a wild maze.
We skip along, no cares to find,
In this haven of the silly kind!

As twilight paints the sky with cheer,
We find ourselves, together here.
In this wayfarer's space of play,
Let joy be loud—come what may!

Whispering Winds of Tomorrow

The breeze tickles, my hair a dance,
Dreams prance around in a silly trance.
Clouds giggle softly, oh what a sight,
Cartwheeling wishes, in pure delight.

Socks on my hands, who needs gloves?
I'll juggle my hopes, like playful doves.
With a wink and a grin, I toss them up high,
Letting them soar, like popcorn in the sky.

A chicken crossed paths, to join the parade,
Chasing my giggles, oh what a charade.
Each flap and each cluck, a hopeful display,
Reminding us all, it's a funny old day.

So let's twirl in the grass, with arms spread wide,
Laughing at worries, let's not let them reside.
With hearts made of sunshine, we skip and we hop,
In this whimsical world, there's never a stop.

Horizon of Hope

The sun yawns big, with a grin so bright,
Taking its time to get out of the night.
Bouncing like bunnies, through dawn's early light,
Chasing all shadows, with giggly delight.

Kites tied to dreams, zoom high in the air,
Whirling and twirling, zest without care.
A toaster just popped, what a breakfast feat,
With laughter as toppings, that can't be beat.

Bananas in pajamas, do a funny jig,
Sliding through slip-ups, oh what a gig.
With jellybeans jumping, dancing so free,
We toss our worries, like leaves from a tree.

So here's to the silly, the wild and the goofy,
We'll paint our horizons in colors so loopy.
With each chuckle and smile, we rise above,
Finding sweet treasures, wrapped in pure love.

Perch of Potential

A squirrel in a suit, with glasses so round,
Ponders the nuts, that he hopes to be found.
From this lofty perch, he looks out with glee,
Dreaming of acorns, as grand as can be.

With a hop and a skip, he dances on air,
Singing to daisies, without a care.
His ambitions are lofty, but oh, what a sight,
For squirrels with dreams can soar into flight.

On branches so high, he plots his next feast,
Where snacks are aplenty, and worries are least.
With each little nibble, potential takes form,
In the heart of the silly, there's always a norm.

So let's all take flight, on this silliness ride,
Gathering hopes, with friends by our side.
With laughter as nectar, we'll sweeten the day,
Finding potential, in the quirkiest way.

Nook of the Serene

In a nook by the flowers, a turtle makes tea,
Whistling sweet tunes, though he's mighty wee.
His kettle is bubbling, with dreams brewed just right,
Sipping on sunshine, oh what a delight!

A cat in a hat offers donuts and cheer,
With sprinkles and giggles that echo quite clear.
Whiskers a-dancing, the laughter spills wide,
In this calm little nook, all worries subside.

With nature's soft whispers, the breeze softly hums,
A symphony sweet, twirling joy that comes.
Each leaf is a note, on this peaceful score,
Reminding us gently, there's always much more.

So take off your shoes, let your worries recede,
Munch on these moments, let silliness lead.
In this cozy little nook, we find it's so clear,
The heart's little treasures, are ever so near.

Threshold of Endless Chances

A crack in the wall, light peeks through,
What's that smell? Is it pizza too?
With a grin like a cat, I lift my foot,
Shall I leap or just stay put?

In this odd hall, socks dance in pairs,
Wearing mismatched shoes, who really cares?
A banana skin waits, a slippery plot,
Will I stumble? I hope not a lot!

Past the new rug, a hamster steals the show,
It's got plans for world domination, you know!
I'm off to the races, feeling quite spry,
But trip on my shoelace, oh my, oh my!

So out through the door, into the wild,
With a joyful heart, and slightly beguiled.
Every step could be clumsy or grand,
But I'll take a chance—life's silly and planned.

Passageway to Serene Horizons

Through a curtain of beads, a frog jumps by,
Looks like he's here for the dance, oh my!
With glittering lights and a disco ball,
I shrug and join in, after all!

A llama in a hat gives a wink,
"Step right up, let's have a drink!"
While sipping lemonade, I trip on a cat,
That's what I get for a smile so flat!

A tapestry hangs, with all sorts of dreams,
But someone misplaced it—by a mile, it seems!
I twirl and giggle, hitting the wall,
But with laughter this big, I'm having a ball!

So forth I will go, with glee in my stride,
Gnarled old trees stand as my guide.
Every twist and turn, a mess or a blast,
Let's hop to the next, let's make this one last!

Gateway to the Soul's Ascent

Underneath a sign that reads 'Free Hugs',
A squirrel in a cape gives me a shrug.
"Is this the way?" I question the air,
He scurries off with a playful flair.

A goldfish barks, "You're going too slow!"
Jumping fishes, what a wacky show!
With a pogo stick, I'm bound to glide,
Or crash into bushes, then crawl to hide!

The walls are all painted in colors so bright,
I wear shades indoors, feeling just right.
With a swing and a miss, I toss my cap,
It lands on a gnome, which makes me clap!

So onward I shuffle, with silly delight,
Skipping past kittens, oh what a sight!
With a wink and a grin, I saunter away,
Each step is a giggle—now what will they say?

Pathway to the Dawning Day

With toaster tongs, I pry open the gate,
A croissant flies out, isn't this fate?
Laughter erupts from a whimsical crowd,
"Breakfast is here! Come dance, be loud!"

The sun's quirk is a dance like no other,
It's wearing a tutu, oh brother, oh brother!
A pancake parade makes its way down the lane,
But here comes a dog with a scarf and a cane!

Chasing my shadow, I run with glee,
Muffins are leaping—can't catch me!
Under muffins' reign, the day takes its flight,
A flurry of giggles bursts forth with delight!

So let's skip ahead to the promise at dawn,
A whimsical world waiting to yawn.
With crumbs on my face and sprinkles in hair,
Every giggle echoes—there's magic to share!

Windowsill of Wishes

In a pot of dreams, a sprout does grow,
It whispers secrets to the moon's soft glow.
With gnarled fingers, I tickle its leaves,
Hoping it'll grow shoes that fit, if it believes.

A squirrel runs by with a tiny hat,
I ask, "Is that stylish?" He twitches, then sat.
We both sip tea from a broken cup,
Giggling at wishes that seem to hiccup.

The sun winks down, a cheeky ray,
"What's a wish without laughter? Come out to play!"
A rainbow slides by on a candy cane,
Telling me dreams can dance in the rain.

So here on this sill, with my pals by my side,
We wait for our hopes to come in with the tide.
Each odd little wish, like a game of charades,
Reveals that the best dreams are never upgrades.

Opening to Tomorrow

A creaky door swings with a groan and a squeak,
I peek through the crack, just to take a peek.
Tomorrow unfolds in a burst of confetti,
With pancakes as big as a bear's fuzzy teddy.

The clock ticks a tune, a weird little beat,
While dancing socks put on quite the feat.
I shout to the world, "Where's my silly parade?"
And a chicken in boots struts in unafraid.

Sunscreen on noses, we're all ready to bake,
With cupcakes for breakfast, oh what a mistake!
But tomorrow's a party, so let's not be shy,
With sprinkles and giggles that touch the blue sky.

The horizon holds promises, all bright and new,
Let's paint it in colors, of every sweet hue.
So open that door, let the laughter invade,
And don't forget cake, if a party's made!

Corridor of Change

In a hall where echoes play tag with the wall,
I chase after shadows that giggle and sprawl.
A poster declares, "New Haircuts Today!"
I fret over scissors then shout, "Hip-hip-hooray!"

Each step that I take on the polka-dot floor,
Comes with a soundtrack—oh, what's that? More!
The ceiling is wiggling, the floor's doing flips,
They're dancing in rhythm, throwing wiggly quips.

The lamps start to wink, a comedy show,
With lightbulbs that joke in a cheeky glow.
I laugh as they bicker about who is bright,
Maybe they'll change me, if I don't take flight.

So let's skip down this hall, let our spirits collide,
With a jest or a pun, oh, what fun to abide!
For change is a joke that we all can embrace,
Let's start a new trend in this wacky old place!

Gateway of Encouragement

A gate swings open, squeaking away,
Behind it, a land of zany display.
With marshmallow clouds and a trampoline stream,
Everyone jumps in, filled with laughter's gleam.

An eagle in glasses gives math tips galore,
"Add a pinch of fun to make life encore!"
We barter bright smiles for marshmallow fluff,
Dealing with giggles, never too tough.

Several trees wear hats, quite whimsical flair,
As they tap dance together, tossing leaves in the air.
"Cheer up! Take a spin! Make your heart do a flip!"
A tuba plays tunes, oh, let's make it hip!

This gate, oh so bright, leads to joy's golden key,
With each little nudge, we shout, "Let it be!"
So step through this portal with friends by your side,
Where encouragement sparkles, and silliness glides!

Portal to a Restored Dream

In a nook sat a cat with a hat,
Dreaming of places, fancy and sprat.
He danced on the ceiling, quite out of style,
Chasing bright beams with an oversized smile.

A window popped open, inviting a breeze,
Tickling noses, oh, such a tease!
Up flew a kite made of jelly on string,
With laughter and giggles, the joy it would bring.

A mouse in a tux gave a wink and a cheer,
Said, "Life is grand, never fear!"
With a hop and a skip, they sang out loud,
In their silly world, they felt so proud.

So when life feels heavy, and dreams start to fade,
Remember the laughter, the fun you had made.
With a wink and a grin, keep your hopes ever bright,
Chase after your dreams, let them take flight.

Pathway to the Heart's Resolve

A penguin on skates, slipping with glee,
Waddled past snowmen as happy as can be.
In a world made of giggles and jiggly pies,
He twirled and he twinkled beneath frosty skies.

Socks lined in colors, oh what a sight,
Each striped and polka-dotted, purely delight!
A parade of the silly stepped out on the street,
Where everyone danced to a rhythm so sweet.

The moon peeked down, chuckling along,
As the people all sang their favorite song.
With hearts full of courage and smiles so divine,
They knew in their bones that all would be fine.

So take up your courage, let laughter ignite,
Embrace all the madness, twirl into the night.
For joy is the fuel that drives every dream,
And laughter, my friend, is a magical beam.

Threshold of Promise

A frog in a suit said, "Time to take flight!"
He hopped on a lily while juggling with might.
His friends in the pond cheered, splashing with fun,
As he leaped through the air, shining bright like the sun.

The crickets composed a whimsical tune,
And fireflies danced, lighting up every room.
They gathered for snacks made of popcorn so sweet,
While sharing silly stories to skip on their feet.

A turtle proclaimed, "Why move with such haste?"
While dozing in sunshine, he savored the taste.
The race may be slow, but the joy is the goal,
With each little chuckle, they nourished their soul.

So swing open the door, let the laughter in,
For a world full of whimsy makes spirits begin.
With daffodils dancing and joy all around,
In each little moment, happiness can be found.

Gateway to Tomorrow

A squirrel wore glasses, all serious style,
Proclaiming a meeting in a grand, silly smile.
With acorns for snacks and tales to unfold,
Together they'd dream, sharing hopes made of gold.

The hedgehogs discussed how they'd sprout tiny wings,
Debating the merits of singing fish swings.
The laughter grew louder as ideas took flight,
In a world full of nonsense, it all felt so right.

A flight of pink turtles, oh, what a sight!
Gliding through puddles, spreading pure light.
With hats made of leaves, they'd dance on the ground,
Spreading joy and laughter, a treasure they found.

So chase after dreams, don't settle for less,
For the journey of laughter is truly a quest.
In the gateway of giggles, tomorrow will bloom,
With hope as your compass, dissolve every gloom.

Outlook of Opportunity

A squirrel in a suit, for a job he does seek,
With acorns in hand, feeling quite chic.
He winks at the cat, who's plotting a scheme,
While dreaming of cheese in his delightful dream.

The mailbox is chubby, with secrets to share,
Each letter a tip for those who would dare.
A stamp with a mustache, how silly and neat,
Whispers of riches, or maybe just sweets.

The sun shines like butter on toast in the sky,
As birds throw confetti—oh my, oh my!
A dance at the corner, the trees start to sway,
Opportunity knocks in a most quirky way.

So off with a giggle, we leap and we smile,
For life's just a circus, let's stay for a while.
With laughter as currency, we'll bank all the cheer,
In this silly adventure, good fortune is near.

Portal of Discovery

A toaster that sings while it browns up some bread,
Calls out to a spoon with a curious head.
They chat about jelly and new peanut spreads,
While a muffin half-falls, claiming laughter instead.

The curtains are gossiping, swaying with flair,
As socks plot escape trips to lands of fresh air.
They dream of new partners, those shoes left behind,
In a world full of colors, delightful and blind.

A cat in a bowtie, with a pirouette twist,
Teaches a goldfish how not to be missed.
Together they leap through a small, shiny hole,
Exploring the depths of a mystical role.

And there on the other side, candy clouds float,
With laughter and wishes all wrapped up in coats.
The portal is open, so join in the fun,
For every odd journey makes two out of one!

Threshold of Joyous Whispers

A gnome with bright pants holds an umbrella high,
To catch all the giggles that tumble from the sky.
He offers a cupcake to a frog in a tie,
Who croaks out a joke that makes all the birds fly.

The flowers are dancing with hats made of cheese,
While ants form a band, bringing everyone ease.
A mouse with a mustache conducts from a shoe,
And everyone hums in a joyfully tune.

Each whisper's a secret, like bubbles in tea,
Floating around in this kooky jubilee.
So gather your laughter, let smiles be your sword,
As we waltz through this magic where no one's ignored.

A sprinkle or two of delight on the way,
Will brighten even the dimmest of gray.
So step through this laughter, let joy take its flight,
In the quirky parade that lasts day and night.

Entry to Unwritten Stories

Beneath an old tree, with a door made of light,
Is a place where the odd things come out for a bite.
A snail plays the trumpet, a rabbit wears specs,
While fishes go dancing, all baffled by T-Rex.

They flip through the pages, left blank, yet so bold,
Each crease holds a secret, a tale to be told.
Bubblegum monsters outwit the grass trolls,
Their antics are silly; they've just rolled their wheels.

Chimneys are chiming with jingles of glee,
As walls whisper tales that are fancifully free.
A duck with a monocle snaps at a joke,
In this place full of sparks, where imagination awoke.

So swing open that door to whichever you dare,
With giggles for currency, adventure's laid bare.
In stories unwritten, where laughter entwines,
You'll find joyful surprises that spark and that shine!

www.ingramcontent.com/pod-product-compliance
Lightning Source LLC
Chambersburg PA
CBHW060111230426
43661CB00003B/157